A PHONIC DICTIONARY

Platt & Munk, Publishers/New York

A Division of Grosset & Dunlap

A PHONIC DICTIONARY

By Linda Hayward • Pictures by Carol Nicklaus

For Bill who thought of the "Eel Page", and for Eric who wanted to change the labels, but we didn't.

1982 Printing

Library of Congress Catalog Number: 80-83588
ISBN: 0-448-47336-4 (Trade Edition)
ISBN: 0-448-13923-5 (Library Edition)
Copyright © 1973 by Platt & Munk Publishers.
Copyright © 1981 by Grosset & Dunlap, Inc.
All rights reserved.
Published simultaneously in Canada. Printed in the United States of America.
(Originally published as *Letters, Sounds, and Words: A Phonic Dictionary.*)

Contents

A Code For Sounds   7

Beginning Consonants: One Sound   9

Beginning Consonants: Two Different Sounds   29

Beginning Consonants: Blended Sounds   35

Beginning Consonants: Special Sounds   63

Beginning Consonants:
    Odd Spellings For One Sound   73

Beginning Vowels:
    Long Sounds And Short Sounds   81

Index   95

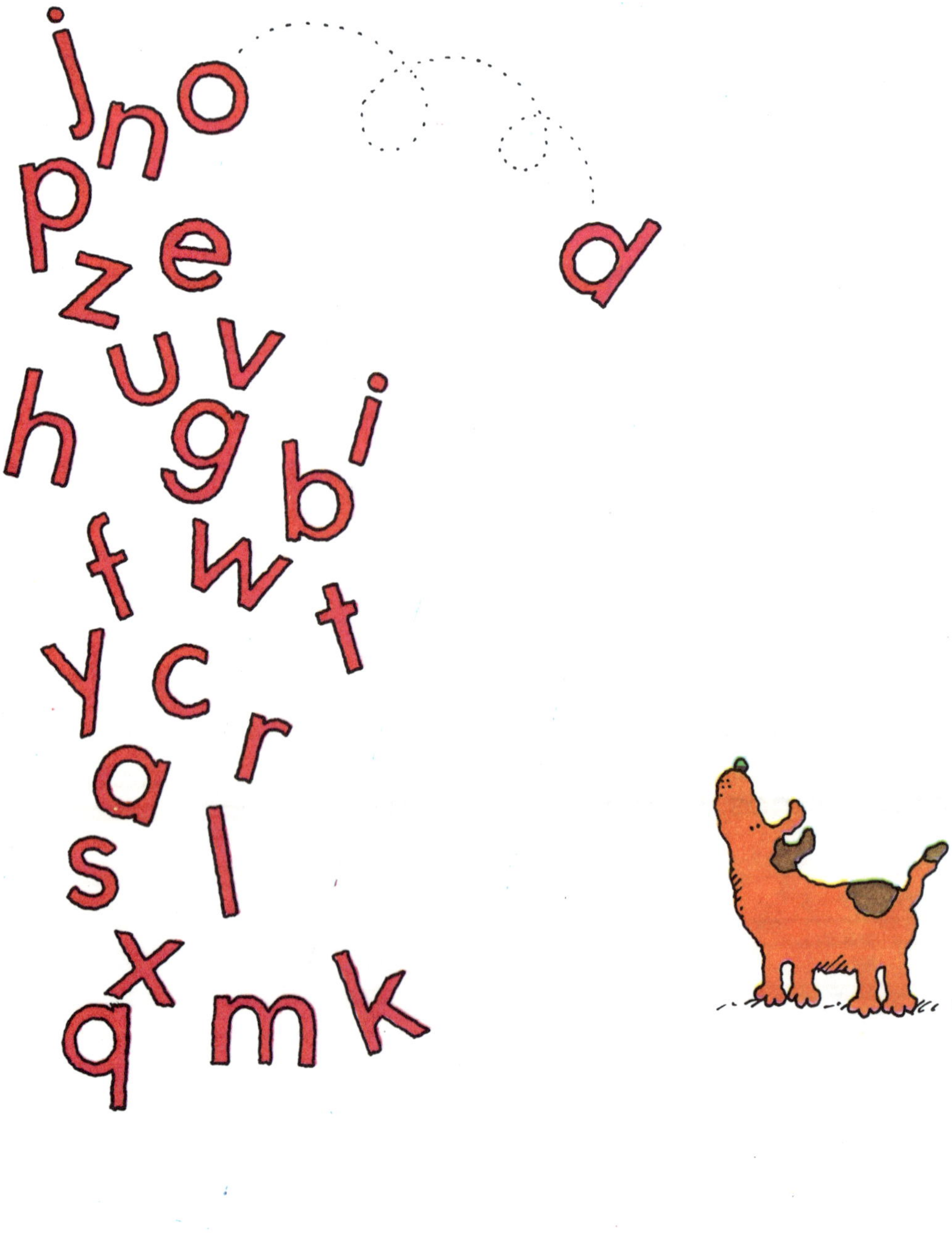
j n o
p
z e
d
u v
h g b i
f w
t
y c
r
a
l
s
x
q m k

A Code For Sounds

When we say words, we make sounds.
We make two sounds to say **at**.
We make three sounds to say **hat**.
Suppose we want to show a word on paper.
We can draw pictures.
We can draw this 🎩 for **hat**,
but how do we draw a picture of **at**?

Suppose we invented pictures for sounds.
It would be a code.
Each picture would stand for a sound.
This picture a
could stand for the first sound in **at**.
This picture t
could stand for the second sound in **at**.
Somebody could look at our pictures,
make the sounds, and say the word.

A long time ago people did this.
They invented pictures for sounds.
The pictures they invented are called letters,
and the letters stand for sounds.
There are only twenty-six letters in the code we use.
We call our code for sounds the alphabet.

Beginning Consonants: One Sound

There are two kinds of letters:
consonants and vowels.
The difference between consonants and vowels
is something like the difference
between bread and peanut butter.
Bread gives shape to a sandwich
but peanut butter holds the bread together.
Consonants give shape to a word
but vowels hold the consonants together.

Consonants can be anywhere in a word.
When a consonant is at the beginning of a word,
it is called a beginning consonant.
Each beginning consonant in this section
stands for one sound.

b

BOOM

BANG

BONG

BONK

BOO BA BA BOO

BOING

BING

bells

bagpipes

bucket

baton

bongos

banjo

baritone bird

box BIRD BAND

book

Bird bands aren't bad,   but books are better.

d

dog

door

dirt

dog digging down

dog digging deeper and deeper

Done digging?

Definitely.

p

purple pansies

poodle

parrot

pirate

pelican   puppy   pink porcupine

peacock

people

potatoes   pony pulling porpoise   panda

Paraders are peculiar, particularly parading potatoes.

q

queen

Quack.

quilt

Queen questions quack.

Quack?

QuackQuackQuack

quick quacks

Quiet!

Quack.

Quackers never quit.

j

juggler juggling jam jars

Jaws!

jaws

juggler in a jam

jam in a jaw

jaws in a jam

y

"YAKETY-YAK!"

"A yard of yellow yarn for your yakety yak?"

"Yes."

a yakety yak

"YAKETY-YAKETY!"

m

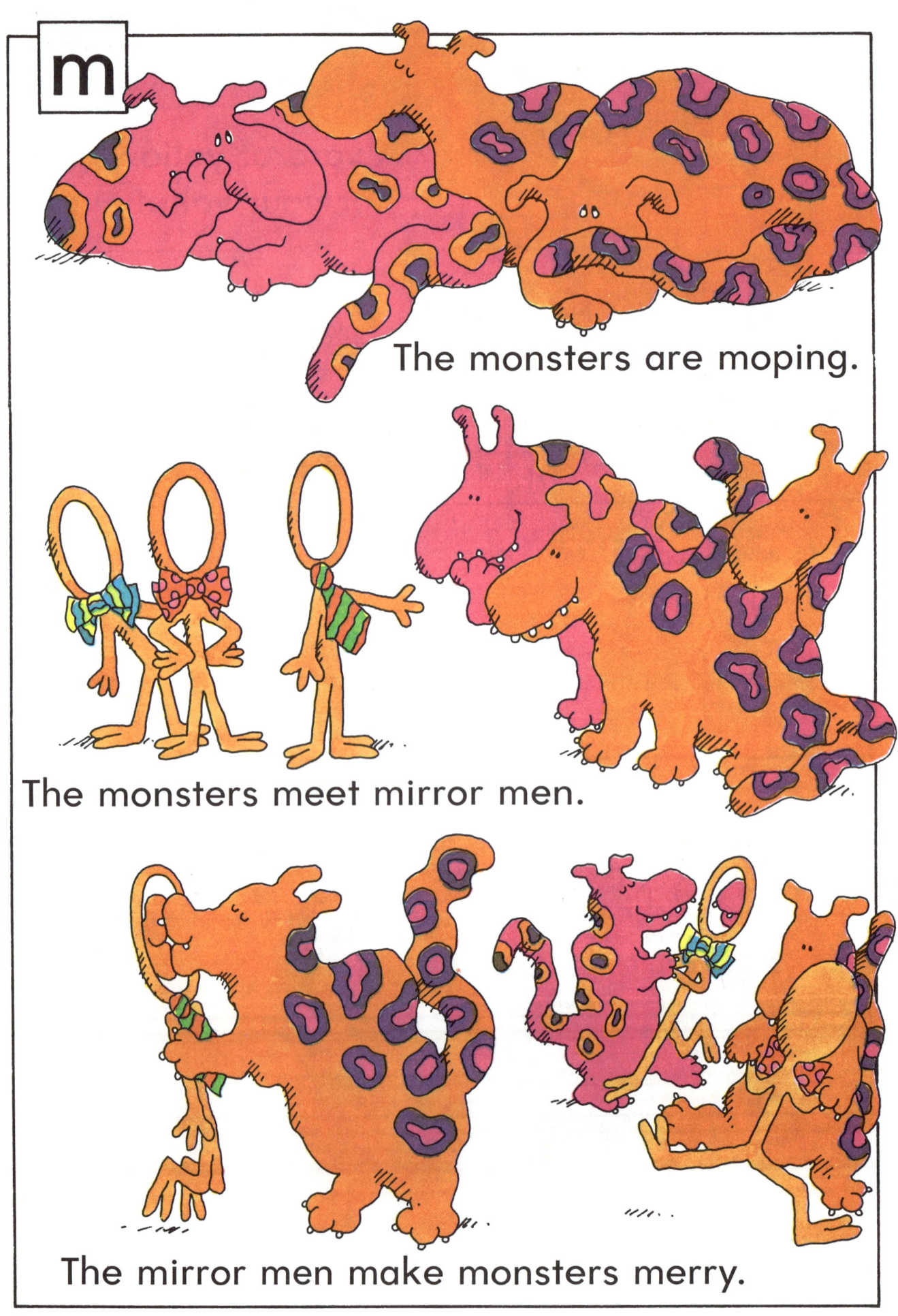

The monsters are moping.

The monsters meet mirror men.

The mirror men make monsters merry.

n

"New neighbor."

"Nice."

"Noisy neighbor."

"Not nice."

"Noise at noon! Noise at night!"

"Nobody needs noise noon and night."

A new neighbor is nice, but no noise nearby is nicer.

17

W

wolf waking

wolf washing

wolf weighing

wolf watering

wolf walking to work in woods

18

V

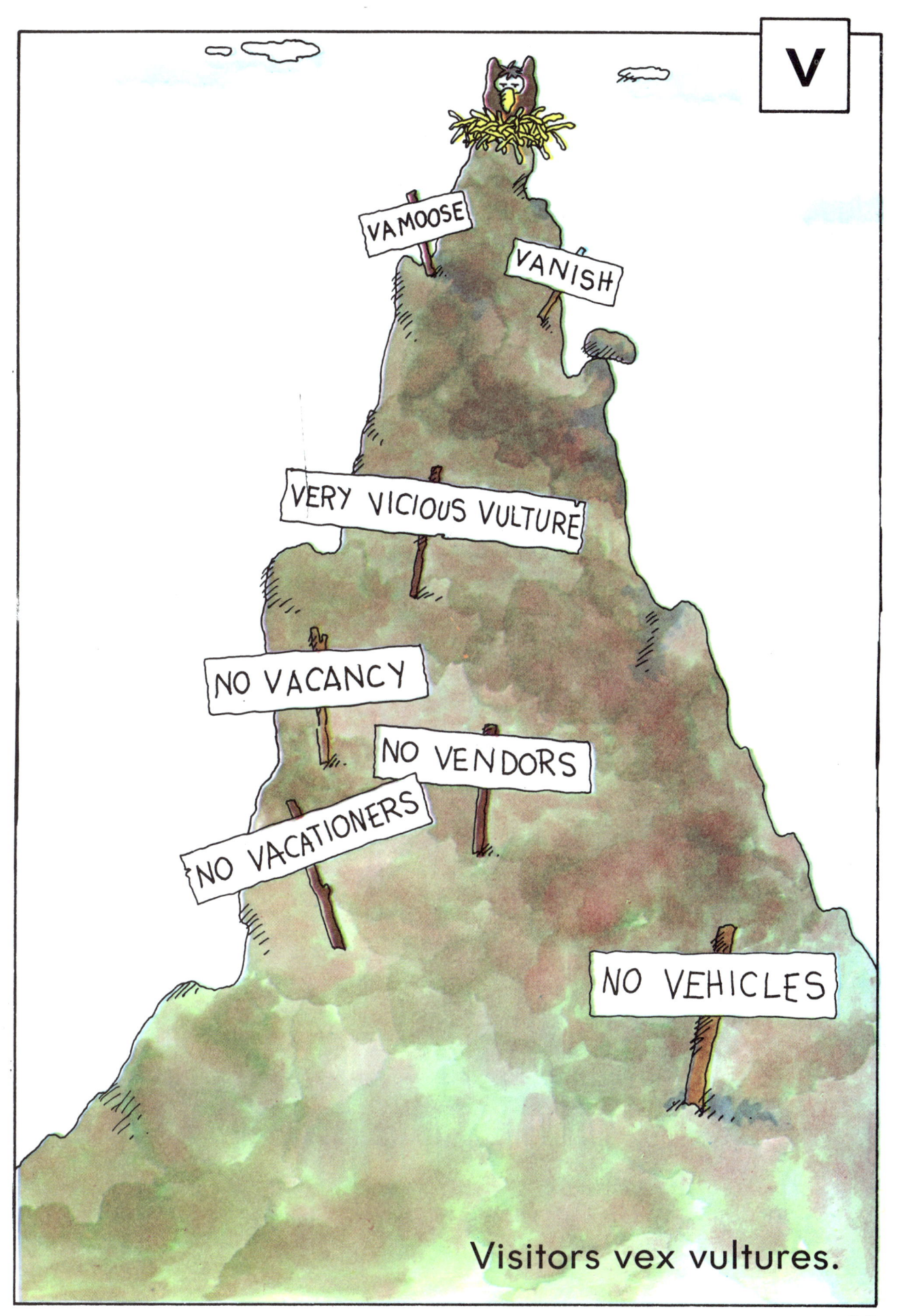

VAMOOSE

VANISH

VERY VICIOUS VULTURE

NO VACANCY

NO VENDORS

NO VACATIONERS

NO VEHICLES

Visitors vex vultures.

r

The rabbits
in red raincoats
in a row
on a raft
in a race
on the river
in the rain
ran
into a rock.

Rocks are rough on racing rabbits.

h

hippopotamus with hat

Hello. Hello. Hello.

a hatching in hippo's hat

HOME

at home on hippo's head

A hippo-home has its hazards.

t

top turtle

turtle tower

ten tiny turtles

Terrific!

TOO TIRED TODAY

TOO TIRED TOMORROW TOO

turtle tucked in tight

turtle taking his time

22

f

fat fish

five fish

four foolish fish

I'm no fool.

fast fish

Fast fish feels fine.

Fat fish feels full.

23

I

A lizard likes to lurk under the leaves.

A lizard likes to lie low on a log.

Lizards are lazy.

Leaping Lizards! A leaping lizard!

k

"Your Kindness called?"

"My kite."

Keeper of the Kites

a kite-kissing king

25

S

sundae

sandwich

sink of soapsuds

sign seller

sailboat

some seed sacks

six socks

So?

26

Z

ZOOM

ZEBRAS

zero zebras in zoo

ZEBRAS

ZING

zigzag zebras

X

DO NOT FEED THE XYLO

xylophone

27

bird	jam	people	six
book	jars	pink	so
box	king	pony	some
but	kissing	potatoes	ten
dirt	kite	pulling	time
dog	leaves	puppy	tiny
done	lie	purple	top
door	likes	queen	turtle
down	lizard	questions	visitors
fast	low	quick	walking
fat	make	quiet	washing
feels	meet	rabbits	wolf
fine	men	race	work
fish	needs	rain	xylophone
five	new	ran	yard
four	nice	red	yellow
full	night	river	yes
hat	no	rock	your
head	noise	row	zebras
hello	noon	seed	zero
home	not	sign	zoo

Beginning Consonants: Two Different Sounds

Each beginning consonant in this section stands for two different sounds.
Usually **c** stands for the same sound that **k** stands for.
Sometimes **c** stands for the same sound that **s** stands for.
Usually **g** stands for a sound no other letter stands for.
Sometimes **g** stands for the same sound that **j** stands for.

One reason we have two pictures for one sound is that people are used to spelling words in certain ways.

C

Can a camel
carrying
a cuckoo on a cushion,
canaries in cages,

carpets,
cases of cabbages,
a canoe,
and a car
be comfortable?

Could he be kidding?

C

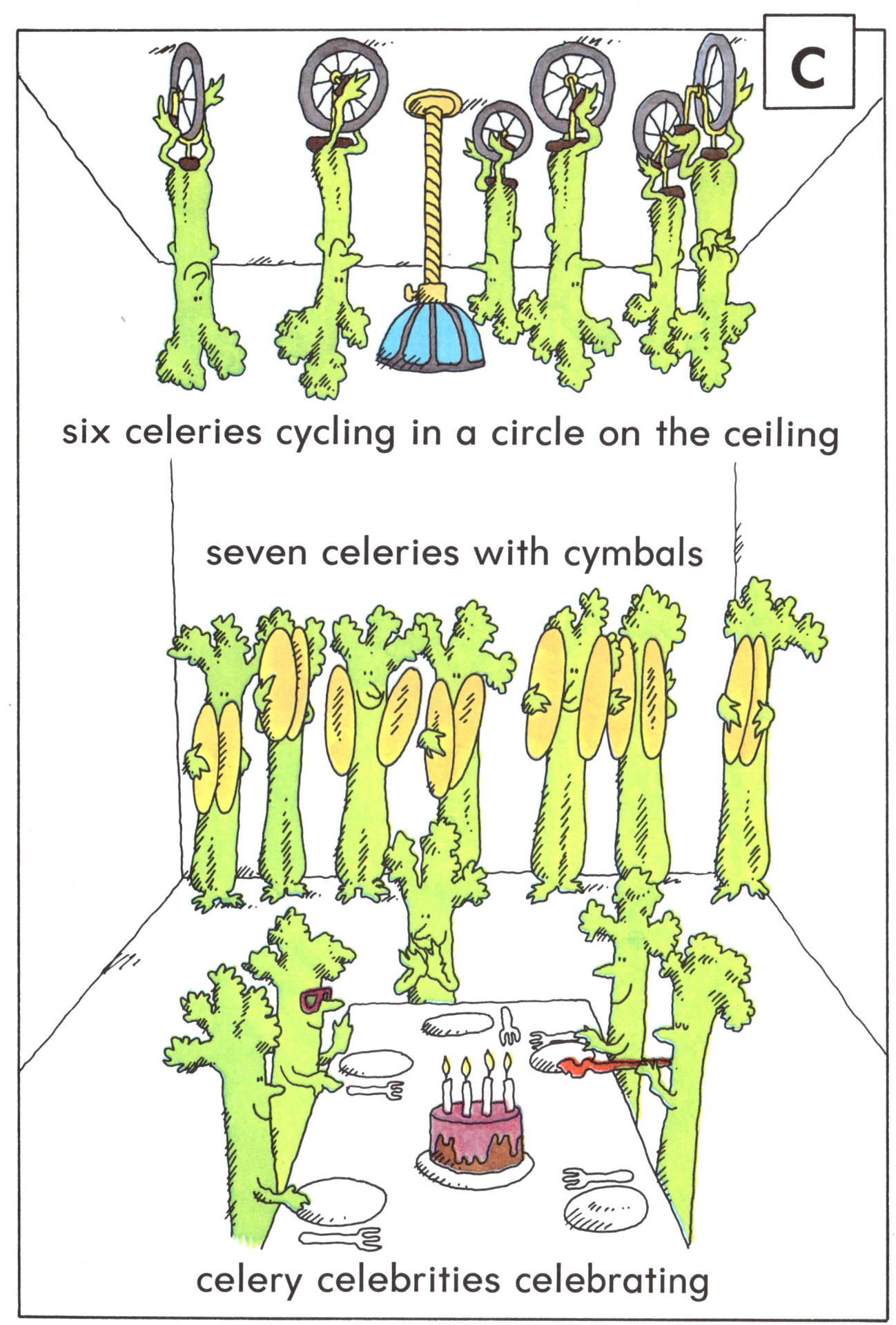

six celeries cycling in a circle on the ceiling

seven celeries with cymbals

celery celebrities celebrating

g

"Ummmm, garbage."

garage goat

"Good."

"GASP" "The garbage is gone."

goat gang

The early goat gets the garbage.

g

a genuine gypsy giraffe

33

cabbages	carrying	cushion	genuine
cages	cases	cycling	gets
camel	ceiling	cymbals	giraffe
can	celery	gang	goat
canaries	circle	garage	gone
canoe	could	garbage	good
car	cuckoo	gasp	gypsy

Beginning Consonants: Blended Sounds

Some words begin with two consonants.
Some words even begin with three.
Two or three consonants at the beginning of a word are usually blended.

In a blend, each consonant stands for its own sound, and the sounds are blended together.
The word **blend** begins with a blend.
The consonants **b** and **l**
come before the vowel **e**.
When you say the word **blend**
you can hear a **b** sound and an **l** sound,
before you hear the **end** of the word.

bl

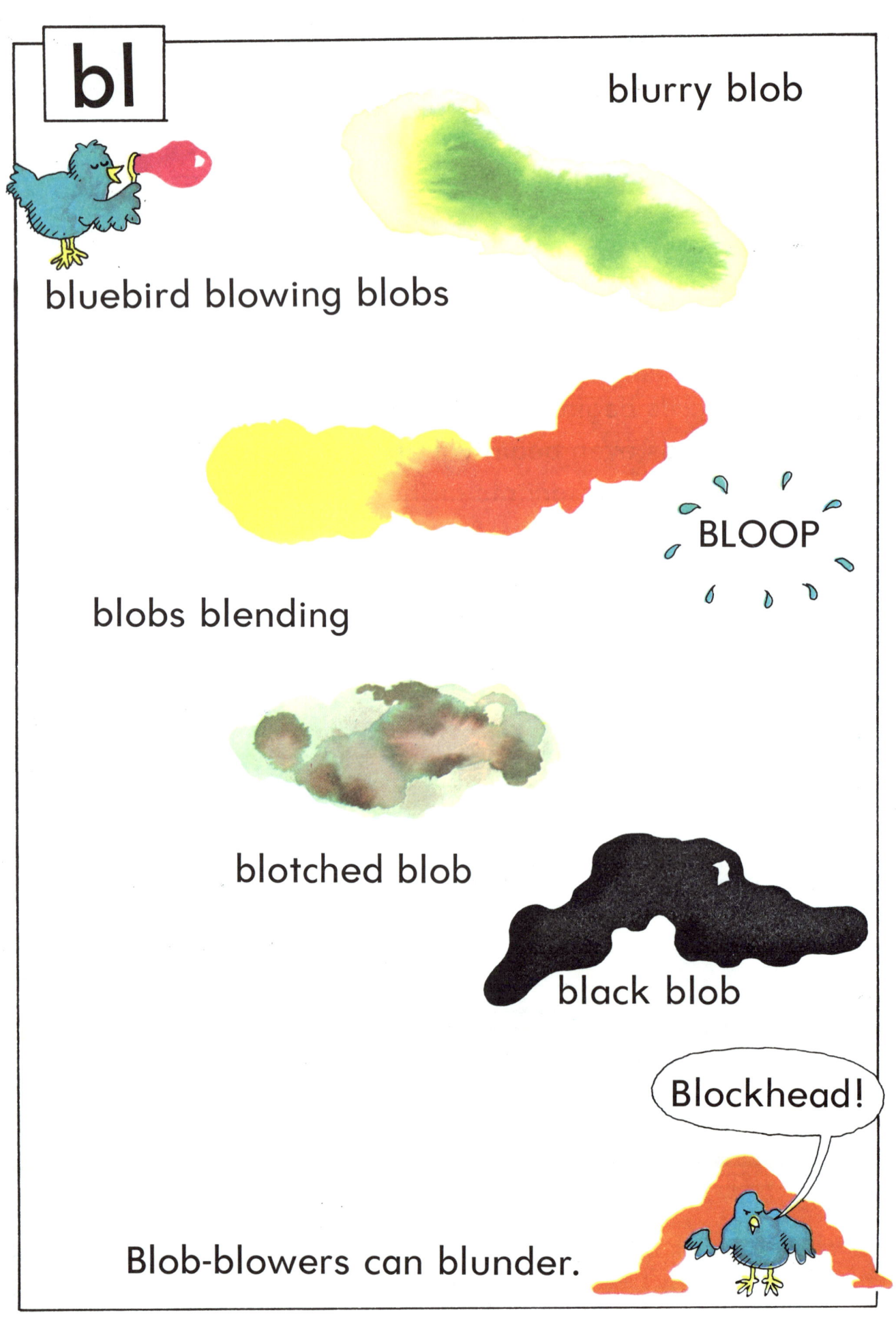

blurry blob

bluebird blowing blobs

blobs blending

BLOOP

blotched blob

black blob

Blockhead!

Blob-blowers can blunder.

br

"Ummmm, brownies for breakfast!"

"Bravo!"

bringing brand-new brooms

"Brilliant!"

brooding over broken broomstick

brownie brew

Brewing briskly breaks broomsticks.

37

cl

CLUNK
CLONK

CLINK
CLUCK

closet

cleaning up clutter

Cluck?

CLUCK

CLATTER

clumsy clucker climbing on clocks

cr

cracker crumbs

CRUNCH CRUNCH CRUNCH

CROAK

Croak?

CROAK

CRASH

CRACKER CRATE

croaker with craving for crisp crackers

39

fl

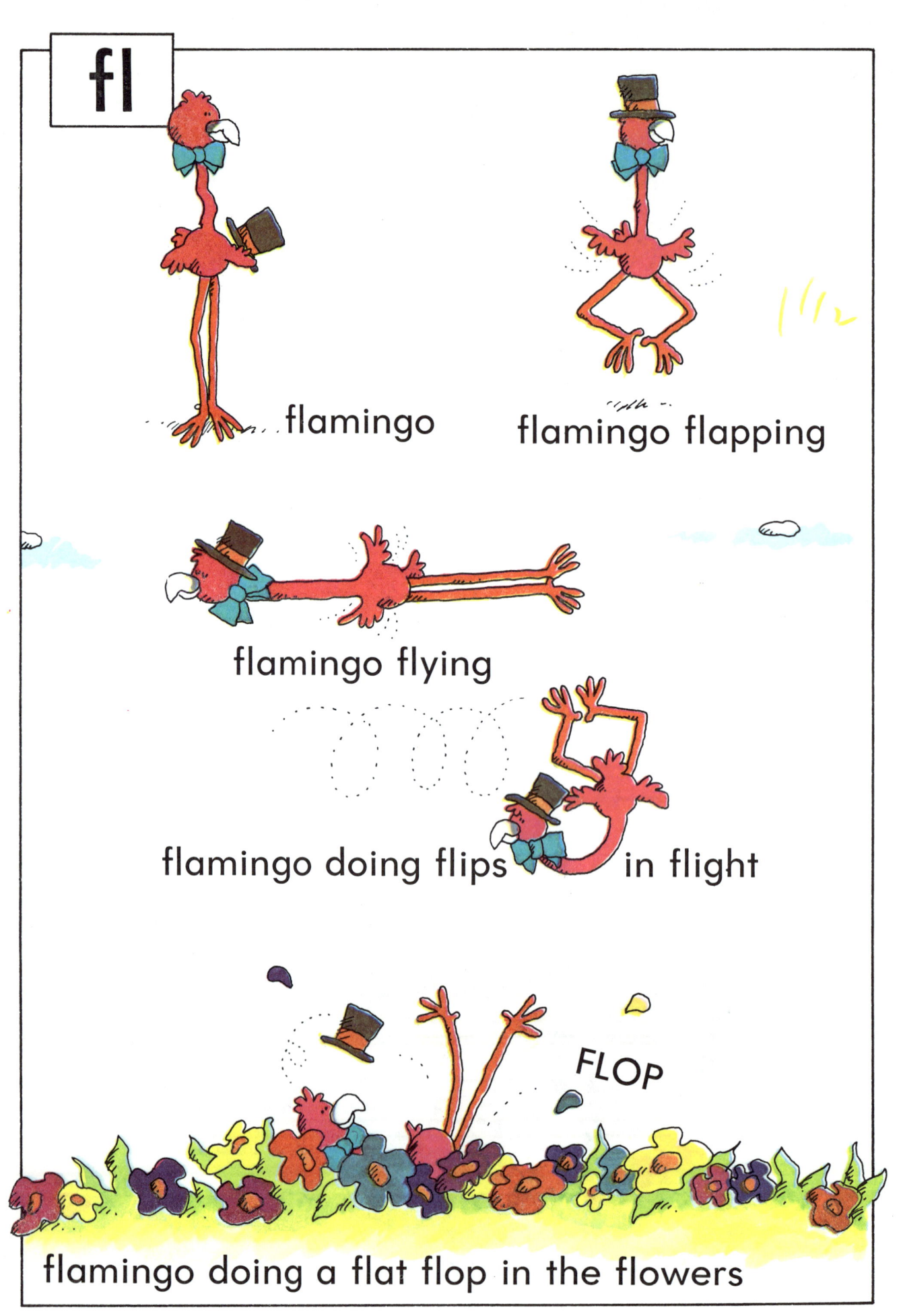

flamingo

flamingo flapping

flamingo flying

flamingo doing flips in flight

FLOP

flamingo doing a flat flop in the flowers

fr

frowning frog

fresh fruit from frog

frolicking to

frolicking fro

frolicking to and fro

frog friends

gl

"I'm glamorous!"

glump

"I'm glorious!"

"I'm glad I'm a glump!"

gr

Grandfather!

Great-grandfather!

Grandson!

Great-grandson!

GROUCH GROUCH GRUMBLE GRUMBLE

Grandma! Grandpa!

Granddaughter!

Grandmother!

groundhogs greeting groundhogs

43

pl

plain plants

plump plants

plunging plants

plopping plants

plums

plaid plants

Playing pleasantly pleases plants.

pr

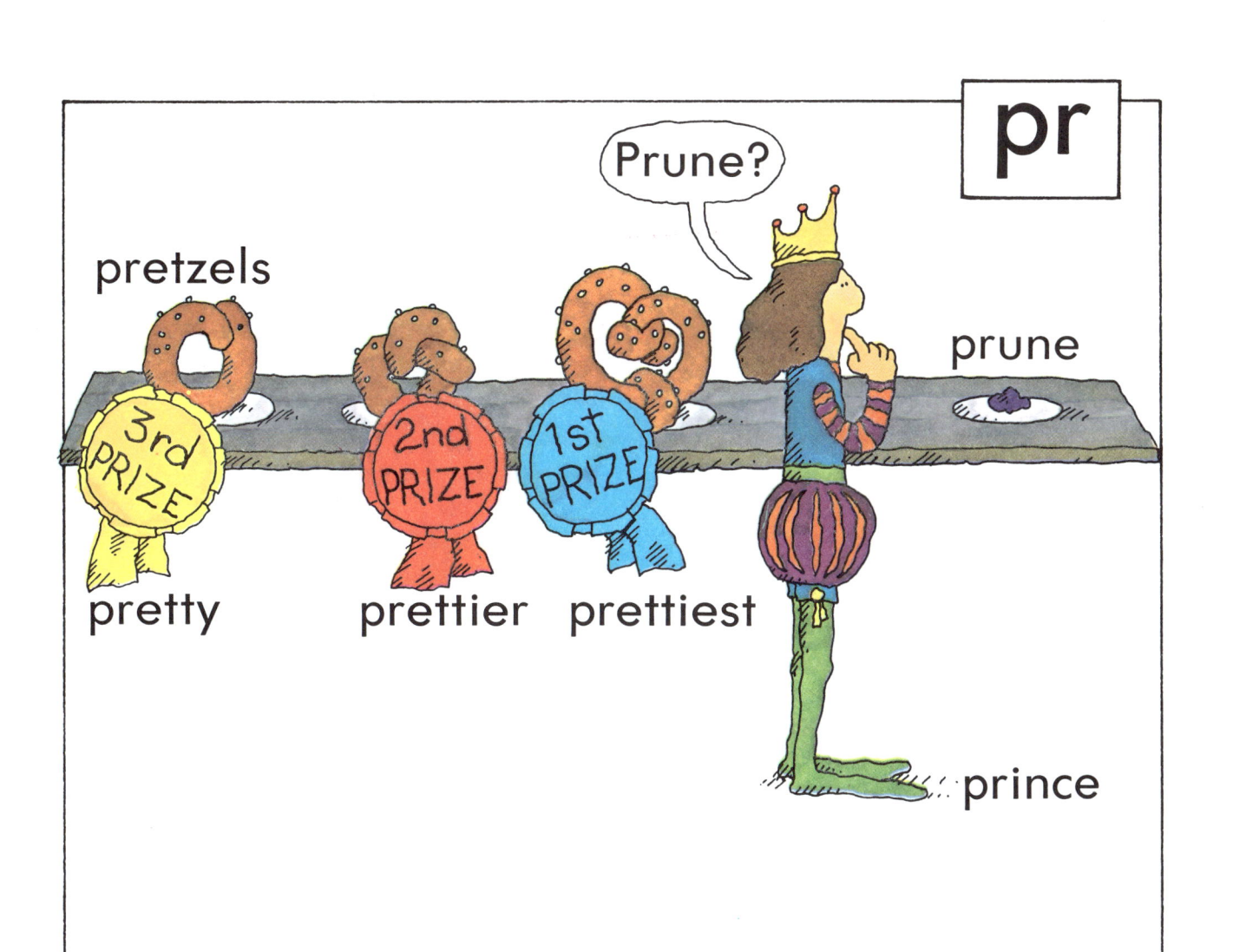

pretzels

"Prune?"

prune

pretty   prettier   prettiest

prince

The prince presents the prize pretzel to the princess.

The princess probably prefers the prune.

dr

The dreaded dragon dreams.

tr

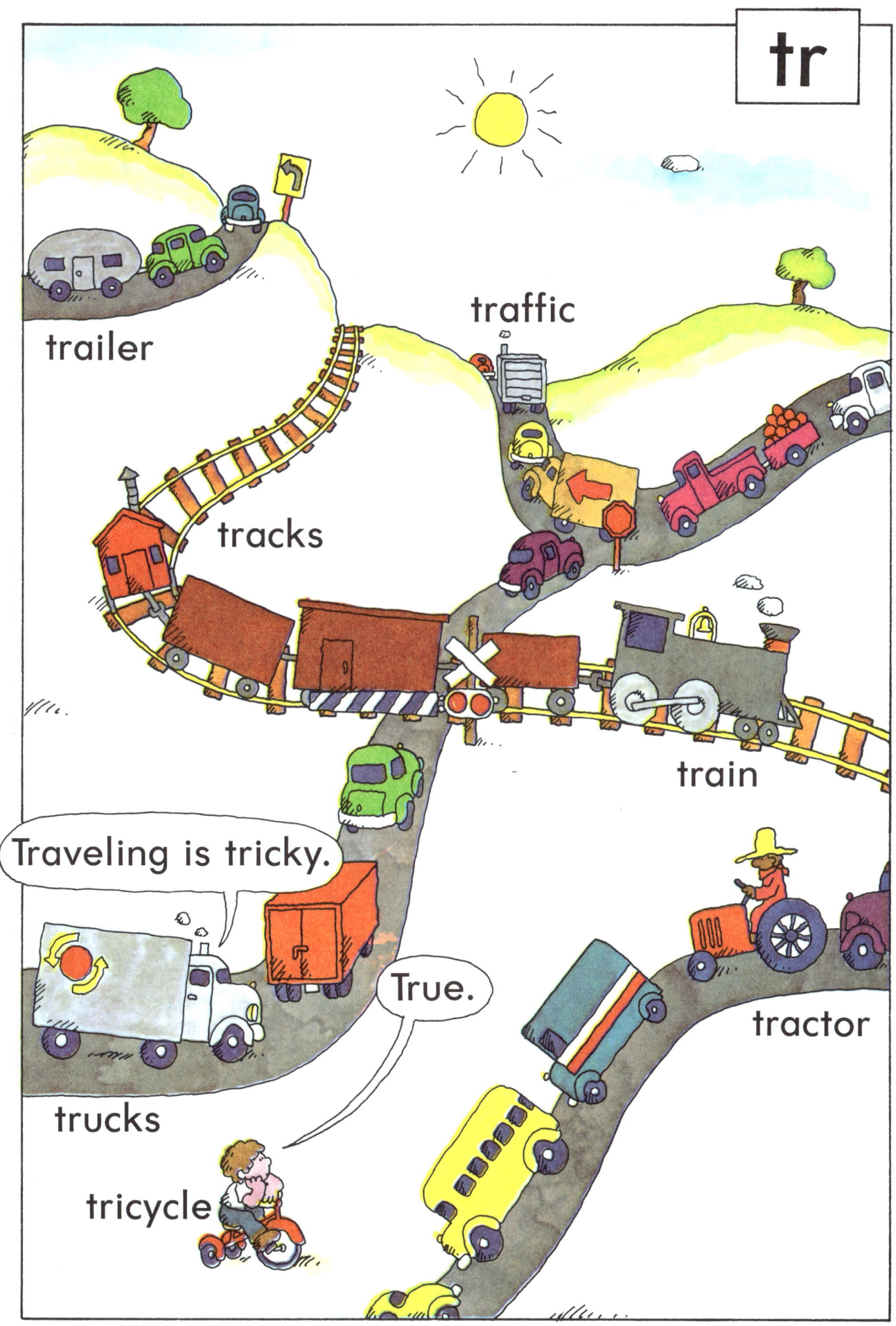

trailer

traffic

tracks

train

Traveling is tricky.

True.

tractor

trucks

tricycle

47

tw

TWEET TWEET TWEET TWEET TWEET TWEET TWEET TWEET TWEET TWEET TWEET TWEET

twelve twins tweeting on twig

twelve twins twirling on twig

twelve twins all a-twitter

sw

swans swimming

SWOOSH

swan in a swift swoop

SWOON

swan's sweetheart in a swoon

swan in a swirl

49

sl

Slippery!

Sloppy!

Sloshy!

Slick!

Slurpy!

Slushy!

Slurpy?

A stork stands on stilts.

Stork starts to stumble.

st

Stupendous!

Steady!

A steady stork stays standing.

51

sn

SNORE

sneakers

Snore?

SNORE

snakes snug in sneakers snatching snoozes

sm

It's smart to smile.

a small, smooth smile

SMASH

a smashing smile

53

sc

scary scooters

The Scariest Scooter Ever

sk

skating skunk

skiing skunk

skipping skunk

sketching skunk

skin diving skunk

A skunk is skillful.

sq

squirrel

SQUEEZE ME

square

SQUEEZE ME

squirrel squeezing square

SQUEAK

SQUEAL

SQUEEZE ME

The squeaky square gets the squirrel.

sp

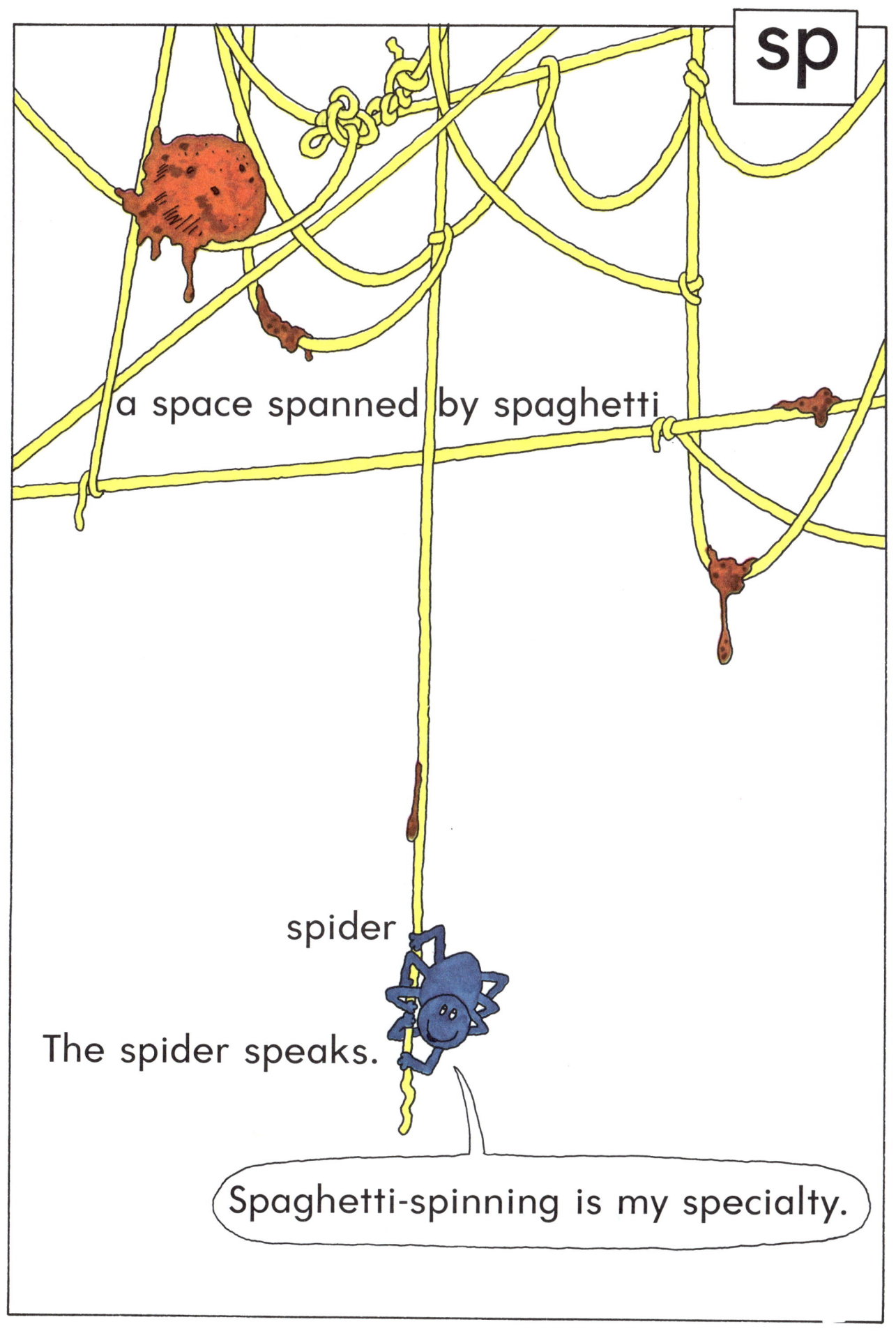

a space spanned by spaghetti

spider

The spider speaks.

Spaghetti-spinning is my specialty.

spl

splits

SPLISH   SPLASH

SPLOSH

Splits make a splendid splash.

spr

sprout

sprinkling sprout

sprout springs up

sprout spreads out

sprout

str

strong strawberry

strong strawberry struggling with string

strikingly strong strawberry

Strength in strawberries is strange.

scr

SCREECH

SCREECH

scrawny screechers

scraps

a scramble over scraps

screechers with scrapes and scratches

black	flying	scratches	square
blob	fresh	screech	squeak
blowing	friends	skating	squeeze
breakfast	frog	skunk	squirrel
breaks	from	slippery	stands
bringing	fruit	sloppy	starts
broken	glad	small	stays
brownies	glamorous	smart	strange
cleaning	grandma	smash	string
climbing	grandpa	smile	strong
clocks	grouch	smooth	swan
closet	grumble	snakes	swimming
crash	plants	snore	tracks
crumbs	playing	space	tractor
crunch	pleases	spaghetti	train
dragon	pretty	speaks	tricycle
dreams	prince	spider	trucks
flat	princess	splash	true
flips	prize	splits	tweet
flop	scary	spreads	twelve
flowers	scrapes	springs	twins

Beginning Consonants: Special Sounds

When pictures for sounds were invented,
there were more sounds than pictures.
There still are.

A few consonant sounds
do not have a letter of their own.
To show these special sounds,
we use two letters together for one sound.
The two letters together
stop standing for their own sounds.
There is no **c** sound or **h** sound
in the word **cheese**.
The **ch** stands for a special sound.
Sometimes special sounds
are blended with **r**.

ch

children

chocolate chunks

children chewing chocolate chunks

champion
chocolate chunk chewer

sh

sheep showering   sheep shampooing

sheep shining shoes

Show me a showered and shampooed sheep
with shiny shoes,
and I'll show you a sheep in sharp shape.

th

THUMP THUMP THUMP THINK

thinking

THUMP THUMP THUMP THINK

a thought

A thief! Of all things!

Thanks.

th

There he is.

That's him.

These are theirs.

Those are theirs.

This isn't theirs!

67

wh

whiz on wheels

What?
When?
Where?

WHEEZE
WHACK
WHINE
WHIRRRR

Why?

68

wh

"Whose is it?"

half a hat

"Whose is it?"

half a hat

"Who is it?"

"Howie,"

"Howie who?"

"Fine, thank you."

a whole hat

thr

Thread thrills
three thrushes
through and through.

shr

SHRINK SHRUB!
SHRIVEL SHRUB!

shrill shrieks

shrub

The shrub shrinker shrugs.

The shrub shrinker shrinks.

champion	showering	thief	whack
chewing	shrieks	things	what
children	shrill	think	wheels
chocolate	shrink	this	wheeze
chunk	shrivel	those	when
shampooing	shrub	thought	where
shape	shrugs	thread	whistle
sharp	thanks	three	whiz
sheep	that's	thrills	who
shiny	theirs	through	whole
shoes	there	thrushes	whose
show	these	thump	why

Beginning Consonants: Odd Spellings For One Sound

There is no **k** sound
in the word **knew**.
Take away the consonant **k**
and the word isn't the same.
Now it's **new**.
Spelling usually follows the code,
but sometimes it's odd.
In the odd spelling **kn**,
only the **n** sound is heard.
In the odd spelling **ph**,
an **f** sound is heard.

Odd spellings may look strange,
but they are used for the same sounds over and over
in many different words.

kn

nine knights

nine knapsacks

nine knobs

nine knocks

Why do knights knock?

Nobody knows.

gn

gnats

gnu

gnats on gnu

Gnu nets gnats.

not nice for gnats

Gnu nets gnu too.

not nice for gnu

rh

A rhinoceros with rhythm is rare.

wr

wren

wreath

wriggling into wreath

wrapped up in wreath

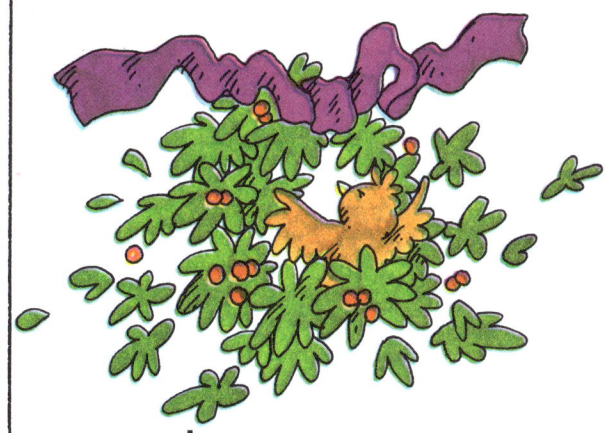

wrestling out of wreath

Wrestling really wrecks a wreath.

ph

phone

The Phantom!

photographer

Phooey!

gh

ghosts

ghastly ghost

ghastlier ghost

ghastliest ghost

ghastly	knobs	phone	wreath
ghost	knock	photographer	wrecks
gnats	knots	rhinoceros	wren
gnu	knows	rhythm	wrestling
knights	phantom	wrapped	wriggling

Beginning Vowels: Long Sounds And Short Sounds

There are only five beginning vowels.
a e i o u
Sometimes **y** is a vowel,
but not at the beginning of a word.
Although there are only five
(and sometimes six) vowels,
there are many vowel sounds.

Each vowel has a long sound
which is the same sound you hear
when you say the name of the letter.
a e i o u
Those are the long sounds.
Each vowel has a short sound, too.
Most of the time a vowel stands for
either its long sound
or its short sound.

Long Sounds

APES →

IVY →

EMU ↑

UNICORN ↑↓

OCEAN ←↑→↓

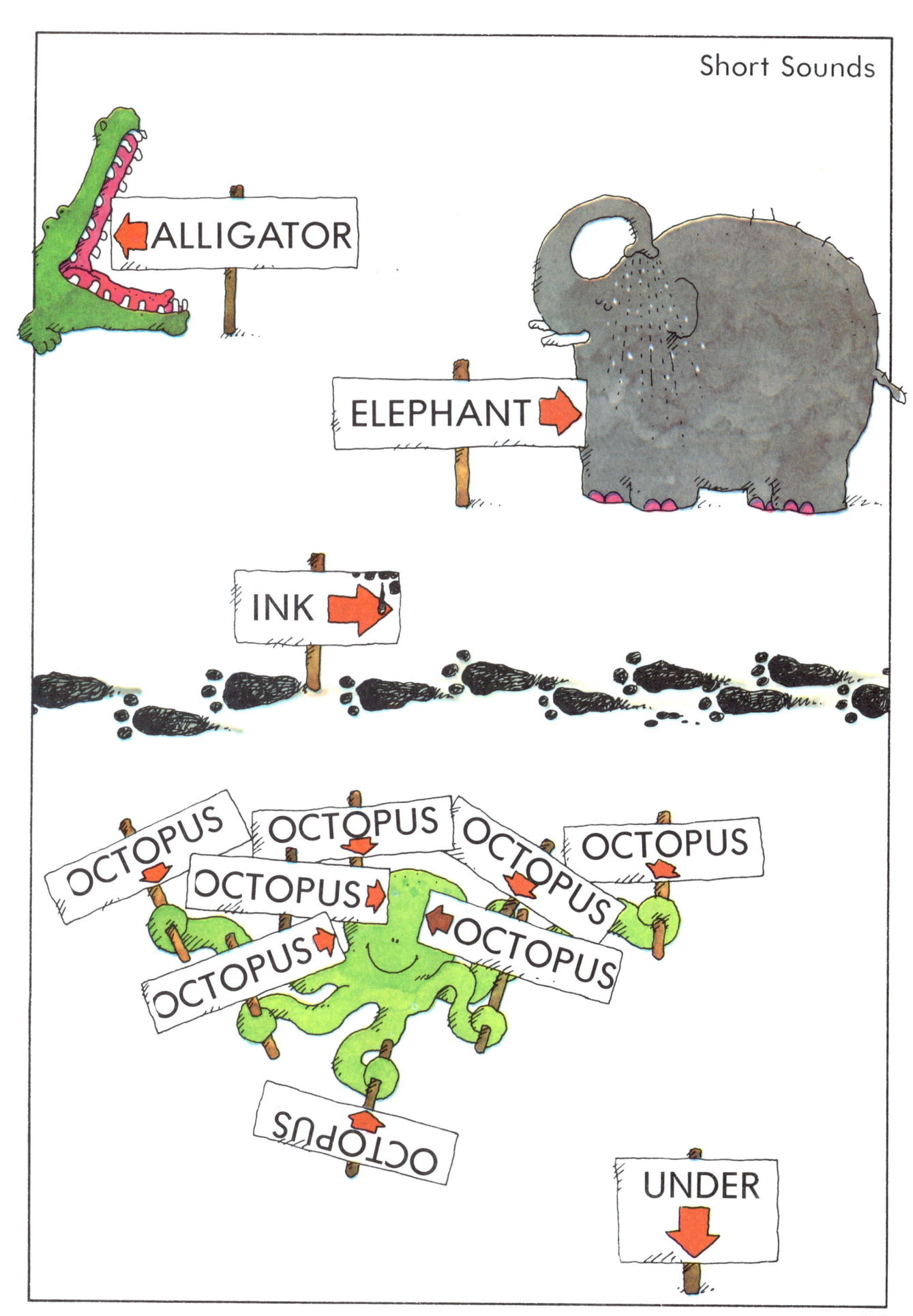

Short Sounds

ALLIGATOR

ELEPHANT

INK

OCTOPUS
OCTOPUS
OCTOPUS
OCTOPUS
OCTOPUS
OCTOPUS
OCTOPUS
OCTOPUS
OCTOPUS

UNDER

83

Long a

ape in apron

acorns in apron

acorns in ape

apron in ape

I ate it.

ache in ape

84

Short a

anteater adding apples

angry anteater angry at anaconda

An anteater is absurd.

anteater admiring answer

85

Long e

"An emu isn't evil."

"An egret isn't evil."

egret   emu

eel

"Eek!"

"Even an eel isn't evil."

86

Short e

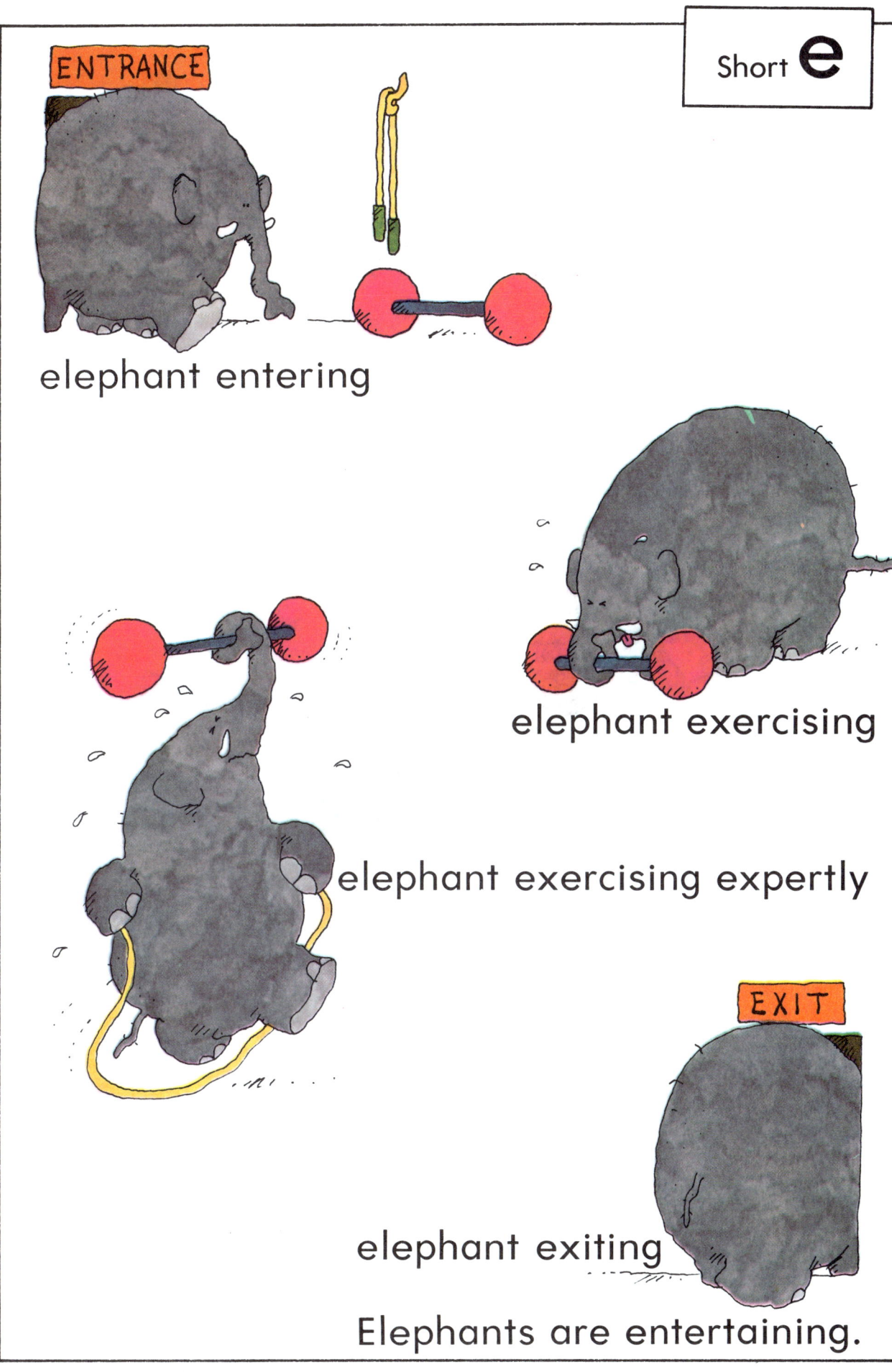

elephant entering

elephant exercising

elephant exercising expertly

elephant exiting

Elephants are entertaining.

87

Long i

idea

ice skates

irons

ice

irons on ice

Irons on ice are not ideal.

Short i

Invention?

It's inside.

It isn't.

It is.

It isn't.

It's invisible.

inventor

investigator

IMPORTANT INVENTION

Inventions are interesting.

Long O

ocean

old overcoat

Ohhhhhhhhh

only overcoat owner in ocean

Short O

octopus
with oxfords on

octopus
with oxfords off

octopus
with oxfords on
and oxfords off

the opposite

Octopuses are odd.

91

Long U

ukulele

using ukulele on unicycle

useless unicycle

useless ukulele

using useless unicycle on useless ukulele

Short U

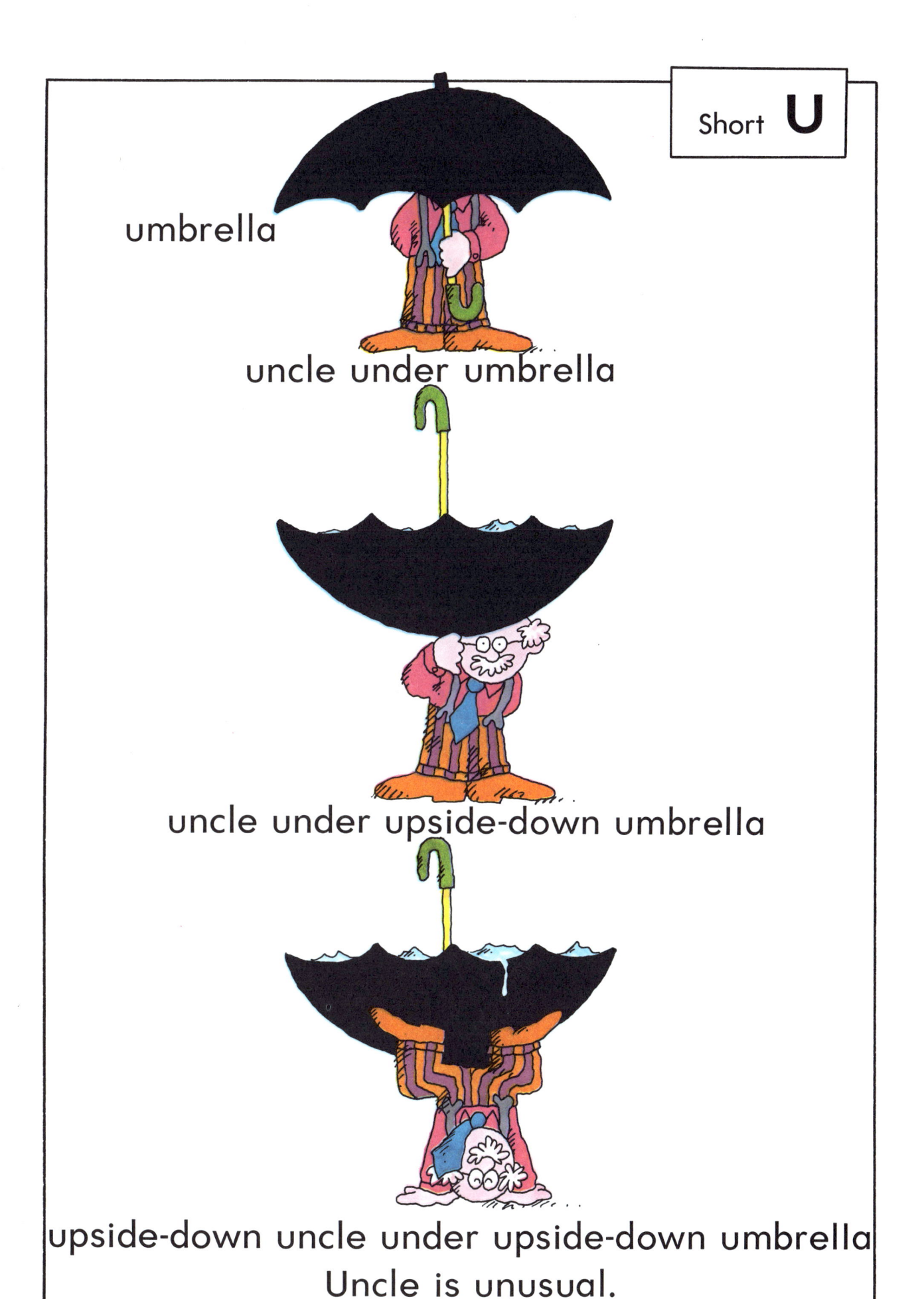

umbrella

uncle under umbrella

uncle under upside-down umbrella

upside-down uncle under upside-down umbrella
Uncle is unusual.

93

adding	entering	invisible	opposite
alligator	entertaining	irons	overcoat
an	even	is	owner
anaconda	evil	isn't	oxfords
angry	exercising	it	ukulele
answer	exiting	it's	umbrella
anteater	ice	ivy	uncle
ape	idea	ocean	under
apples	ideal	octopus	unicorn
apron	ink	odd	unicycle
at	inside	off	unusual
ate	interesting	old	upside-down
eel	invention	on	useless
elephant	inventor	only	using

Index

a /ā/ 84
a /ă/ 85
b 10
bl 36
br 37
c /k/ 30
c /s/ 31
ch 64
cl 38
cr 39
d 11
dr 46
e /ē/ 86
e /ĕ/ 87
f 23
fl 40
fr 41

g /g/ 32
g /j/ 33
gh /g/ 79
gl 42
gn /n/ 75
gr 43
h 21
i /ī/ 88
i /ĭ/ 89
j 14
k 25
kn /n/ 74
l 24
m 16
n 17
o /ō/ 90
o /ŏ/ 91

95

p	12	st	51
ph /f/	78	str	60
pl	44	sw	49
pr	45	t	22
q	13	th /th/	66
r	20	th /TH/	67
rh /r/	76	thr	70
s	26	tr	47
sc	54	tw	48
scr	61	u /ū/	92
sh	65	u /ŭ/	93
shr	71	v	19
sk	55	w	18
sl	50	wh /hw/	68
sm	53	wh /h/	69
sn	52	wr /r/	77
sp	57	x	27
spl	58	y	15
spr	59	z	27
sq	56		